Alone at the Window

Also by Judith E.P. Johnson

Mountain Moods (VDL Publications, 1997)
Gatherers (VDL Publications, 1998)
Fragments (VDL Publications, 2000)
Selected Poems CD (7 RPH, 2001)
Snapshot (Regal Press, 2003)
Landmarks (Ginninderra Press, 2005)
Between Two Moons (Ginninderra Press, 2015)
Waking From Dreams (Ginninderra Press, 2016)

Judith E.P. Johnson

Alone at the Window
haiku & senryu

Acknowledgements

Special thanks are due to my cousin Janet Baker, who makes things happen; to Peter Macrow for his guidance and inspiration; to John Fast for computer advice; and to Lyn Reeves for editing this book.

The author's haiku and senryu, some of which are included in *Alone at the Window*, have appeared in the following publications:
Famous Reporter, *Tasmanian Times*, *poam*, *paper wasp*, *Blue Giraffe*, *Shamrock* (Dublin), *Haiku Oz*.

Alone at the Window: haiku & senryu
ISBN 978 1 74027 720 4
Copyright © text Judith E.P. Johnson 2012
Cover based on a photo by Graeme L. Johnson

First published 2012
Reprinted 2016

GINNINDERRA PRESS
PO Box 3461 Port Adelaide 5015
www.ginninderrapress.com.au

To Graeme
for our life together,
our children
Karen, Debra and Craig
and our little grand-daughters,
Emily and Jasmine.

Introduction

The origin of English-language haiku lies in the hokku of twelfth century Japanese link-verse poetry. The original Japanese 5-7-5 syllable count and the three-line form have changed to accommodate differences in English and to maintain brevity. There is no preamble or explanation.

The haiku is instantly recognisable in, not the Aha! but the Oh! of the haiku moment. This is achieved, in part, by 'surprise in overlooked beauty' (Peter Macrow), and by 'internal connections' (Lee Gurga). The subject matter varies, of course, with the individuality of each poet, but seasons and nature are an important basis of their appeal.

The senryu, however, is mainly about people. If a poem lacks the impact of the haiku moment, it is not a haiku but something else altogether.

Due to its accessibility, the haiku is very popular worldwide in the twenty-first century and gives many readers great pleasure. Personally, I rarely read more than ten haiku at a time. I like to savour them so that they remain with me. They illuminate in my mind and take my breath away with the joy of a haiku moment.

          Judith E.P. Johnson

pre-dawn light
soft on the air
the smell of spring

high tide
flowing over the midden shells
moonlight

she-oak shadows
on the beachside plaque
old tribal names

through apple blossom
the hum
of a plane

church wedding
the curate
catches the bouquet

squalls
some of the rain
is the sea

night breezes through the open doorway full moon

Kangaroo Island

small plane banks –
the sudden cackle
of crated chooks

breakers rolling up the beach fur seals

sitting outside
the Kingscote pub
the concrete mermaid

home again
I find a seashell
in my pocket

photograph
of lagoon reflections –
which way is up?

morning mist
the sea eagle
circles the bay

spindly jetty
the cormorant
in bent reflections

busy road
sparrows drinking
from the stone trough

dusk darkening
in lagoon reeds
black swans

autumn
again in the walnut tree
the white cockatoos

moonlit river
the night of departure
in your eyes

pushing past me
on the empty street
the wind

bedside lamp
behind closed curtains
the moon

awake
in the darkness
the wind

sudden rain
through the dark trees
silver moon-showers

after rain
rain falling
leaf to leaf

Cornelian Bay

on my mother's coffin
roses
from her garden

July dawn – scattering her ashes the wind

stone angel
on the old grave
wing shadows

after her funeral
my mother
in my shadow

dusk –
a rabbit comes out
of a broken grave

fog
I take
the old path home

white Christmas
the bottle of dinner wine
chills in the snow

candlelit dinner
reaching for the wine
my shadow

cool night
the warmth
of sun-dried sheets

forty years on
drawers still lined
with wedding gift wrap

winter solstice –
in my kitchen
bottled boats and potted palms

sunlit river
ripple after ripple
flashes gold

twilight party
how young they look
my old friends

winter night
the house darkens
to one lighted room

midnight lake
floating in the reeds
the moon

crying child
in my arms
her heartbeat and mine

unsteady on its feet
new-born lamb
in falling snow

up early
only the dog
tells me what to do

opening an old picture book
my childhood
fingerprints

shelf ornaments
linked by spider's web –
spring sunlight

toys everywhere
the toddler
puts my cup on the sink

sun
glowing on the chair
the ginger cat

morning birdsong
at the open window
caged canary

holding open
the old shed door
the jasmine vine

grandchildren away
Grandpa watches Playschool
alone

Anzac Day
the Last Post fills the air
with seagulls

between the pines
the moon
on your grave

Northern Territory

honey scent
covering the red sand
desert flowers

didgeridoo –
vibrating on the air
bird wings

desert night
against stars
the earth's curve

sunset
the changing colours
of Uluru

tour bus
all day
the one straight road

away from home
missing
the mountain

fourth-floor balcony
we wave to the man
in the hot air balloon

park café
the peacock
picks up the crumbs

flickering sun
in leaf shadow
butterflies

evensong
birds settle
in the cathedral trees

alone in the crowd
the touch
of your hand

revolving restaurant
slowly the mountain
comes and goes

rain clearing – blue sky in a puddle

incoming tide
the castle
collapses into sand

hushed voices
in the old forest
trees marked for logging

bookshop café wall to wall the smell of coffee

book in hand
the toddler
backs up to my knee

woman breastfeeding –
the old man
pats the baby's head

tea and scones
after The Hallelujah Chorus
small talk

seniors' concert
eighty-eight-year-old sings
Younger than Springtime

westerly gale
all the windfall apples
against the fence

gone ten years
still in my head
my mother's voice

at the airport – saying goodbye again we hug again

alone at the window full moon

www.ingramcontent.com/pod-product-compliance
Lightning Source LLC
LaVergne TN
LVHW021745060526
838200LV00052B/3474